FREE VERSE EDITIONS

Series Editor, Jon Thompson

Free Verse Editions represents a joint venture between *Free Verse: A Journal of Contemporary Poetry & Poetics* and Parlor Press. The series will publish three to five books of poetry per year. We are especially interested in collections that use language to dramatize a singular vision of experience, a mastery of craft, a deep knowledge of poetic tradition, and a willingness to take risks. As the series title suggests, the series is oriented toward free verse, but we will happily consider poetry written in traditional forms. Collections should have individual poems published in well-known journals. We will read collections that do not have a track record of publications, but it is unlikely that they will be accepted for publication.

For more information about the series, visit the series website: see http://www.parlorpress.com/freeverse/index.html. The *Free Verse* journal is on the Web http://english.chass.ncsu.edu/freeverse/

A Map of Faring

Also by Peter Riley

Love-Strife Machine (1969)
The Linear Journal (1973)
Lines on the Liver (1981)
Track and Mineshafts (1983)
Snow Has Settled . . . Bury Me Here (1997)
Passing Measures: Selected Poems (2001)
The Dance at Mociu (2003)
Alstonefield: A Poem (2004)
Excavations (2004)

A Map of Faring

Peter Riley

Parlor Press
West Lafayette, Indiana
www.parlorpress.com

Parlor Press LLC, West Lafayette, Indiana 47906

Library of Congress Cataloging-in-Publication Data

Riley, Peter.
  A map of Faring / Peter Riley.
    p. cm. -- (Free verse editions)
  Includes bibliographical references.
    ISBN 1-932559-59-0 (pbk. : acid-free paper) -- ISBN 1-932559-60-4
(hardcover : acid-free paper) -- ISBN 1-932559-61-2 (Adobe eBook) 1.
Europe--Poetry. I. Title. II. Series.
  PR6068.I4M37 2005
  821'.914--dc22
                                    2005012523

Printed on acid-free paper.

Cover photograph by Beryl Riley

Cover design by David Blakesley

Parlor Press, LLC is an independent publisher of scholarly and trade
titles in print and multimedia formats. This book is also available in
cloth and Adobe eBook formats from Parlor Press on the WWW at
http://www.parlorpress.com. For submission information or to find out
about Parlor Press publications, write to Parlor Press, 816 Robinson St.,
West Lafayette, Indiana, 47906, or e-mail editor@parlorpress.com.

CONTENTS

ACKNOWLEDGMENTS

Sett One, Sett Two, and *Coda* have appeared on three websites: *Sett One* on *Masthead* (Alison Croggan), *Sett Two* on *Jacket* (John Tranter), *Coda* on *Great Works* (Peter Philpott). Individual poems have appeared in *Near Eastern Review, TriQuarterly, Chicago Review,* and *The London Review of Books. The Towns Along the Tisa* and a prose version of *Kalotaszeg* are included in my book of sketches of Transylvania, *The Dance at Mociu,* published by Shearsman Books 2003. The editors publishers and webmasters responsible are warmly thanked.

Noon Province was published in a provisional edition of 150 copies by Poetical Histories (Cambridge) in 1989. It was next published in a bilingual edition with translations by Lorand Gaspar and Sarah Clair, in *Noon Province et autres poèmes,* Atelier La Feugraie, Saint-Pierre-la-Vielle (France) 1996. A selection of 18 pieces was included in *Passing Measures,* Carcanet 2000.

A version of *Noon Province* was presented to Douglas Oliver inscribed "A reminiscence of Europe for Douglas Oliver, on his departure" in February, 1988.

A Map of Faring

First Sett

Crucifix and lamp niche carved in the wall
quiet breathing slowly devolving thought
wine corks and olive pips in the ash heap
soft singing, dry powder, global home.

Prevent me from disheartening, spread
my thought into result seal my song
in a small pot my heel turning on the ground
at the centre, where the sky sits.

Night closes in, heat lifts from the valley floor
the stars reappear, the grasses part
and they enter the earth, the sung men.
The traders, burdened with a constant elsewhere.

Crucifix and oil stoup
in the gritstone wall
a floating wick, turning
shadows. The book
sings itself into the sack of grain
the owl at the door
and the washing-up to be done.

Gladly, willingly, free of guilt
free of not-guilt, fixing
sequences across
distant points, where
shadows gather, where
the living trade, and sing
their lives into the earth.
Everything I do is that song's descant.

The broken pot in the grave
outside the front door
what you might wish to become:
shadows on the sea,
stronghold sure.

Cross and cup scooped
in the living stone
in the earth, elsewhere.

For equity, for spread of gain
raise the white stone, the red
light on the shore where
the merchant ship rounds the headland

Two pale lines on the ground
over the hill's shoulder
the returning workman catches
the song in the night
from the wooded hillside
a faint light among the trees,
owl and badger signalling
beyond their species.

Intimately, in the village, turn
the dance, the baby's head towards.

Face gazing down, rush-light flame
marking eyebrows, inscribed into
the material as if through it,
from somewhere else.

Singing teacher, from somewhere else,
come and sing to me
down the ploughed fields
where the lapwings gather,
the incline, sing to me the elsewhere,
the outcome,
make it plain for all.

The incline, the outcome, I
mislaid a life. But a small light among foliage
strikes the happy lads on the way home,
slowly falling to earth.

Human image, arms outspread—sign
of welcome, pain, abandon, chiselled
into hard earth and held in the cup
a floating light. Hierusalem, slaughtering
ground, turn and see.

I should be modern. The transport passing
overhead in the night, bearing trouble
to the ends of the earth. I cannot
be modern.

It remains with us,
everything we did that
mattered, everything we didn't do that
might have helped.
Pasts accumulate upon us like shining clouds.
We nourished a deaf white cat,
Adrienne and I. When it died we

The pictures on the wall, I can't
remember the pictures on the wall
you shadows, reaching
into life.

Every day at six the mill girls passed the window
their clogs clattering on the stone streets
calling and singing, six day week.

Walk with us, take your part,
the need that cannot perish
that no plenty can ever sate
perches for a second on
the welcome tree and flies into the dark

The dark land wrapped round us,
the shame of injustice and exactly why.
Nearly said so, but didn't, flew.
A life spent avoiding saying

And it says itself, the thin glass around the flame,
the final contract, dawn on shop corner.

Small light in cave wall
floating flame in a pool of oil
above it some joker, some
punished man.

Love's punishment in the tall tower
what is it? to see the world stalking itself . . .

The men come home over the hill
carrying wood for the fire, toys
for the baby, the women do so too
it is considered right to laugh and fuck.
By the owl too, calling
out of its food chain
and the nightingale all day long.

With my singing hand I rummage
echoes in the burnt archive, the dust of
forgotten signatures. There was
fair term in the original prospectus,
the welcome that constructs a town.
Phosphorescence in the sea, and the sky
open overhead. Same old tune,
we yearn for a fair and honest earth.

All the birds know it by heart.

Chiaroscuro. Not a luxury.
A labour, picking at the rock
for years, slowly realising
a quick thought. That there is
someone.

But there was no one.

Thumb-sucking question. They
come fast on all sides, the fat workers
tiring themselves on the land and its outcome

Its incline, naturally. I love
that faint lack in the air when
the light stoops over the trees and
shrinks to a pale rectangle.

And the actively innocent,
the victims, for whom there is no one.

Shout of joy in death dump.
Cross and point, as on a map.
Lights converging to a town.

The image stands out from the wall,
solid, indicative, moves
almost. The earth moves.
The body fades. Is helped
into the earth.

"Sheltered by yew trees" and below,
by the track, damsons. *Ten
thousand years, drinking of the wine.*
Messages of hope from beseiged caves.
Poppy, moth, and candlelight.

Swish of car tyres passing in the night, in the rain,
minor A road over a Suffolk heath, light
beams into the leaking cloudbase and folds back down
and over they go for home, one after another, thousands
of homes, somewhere or never, refrigerators, hope.

And above, in the head arc, frightful machines,
in the speculation zone, above the clouds, star calipers
sharpened to a point, closing. Shout of joy or pain where
Africa turns back, and Arabia weeps
for her lost children. Clipping the heart.

Christ against the living tree
cut in stone, sunk
into hardheartedness.

A few olives in the late evening, and red wine,
saying the word, Africa,
into the night.

And starting up the song, that forgets suffering
completely. My poor mind, it says,
turns on the spot, in the glow of the world.
My alcohol and daisy brain.

Then says that other word, Rwanda,
into silence.

The hard heart breaks, the wax heart melts,
the final heart uncoils.

The terminated man, ghosted by light,
realised by light, thin taper
in a niche in the wall, Y-shaped shadow.

At night the stars gyrate on the axis
of the village plan, a cluster of poor huts
in miles of scrub. Sleep secure,
night bird on the roof-ridge
proclaiming common fate.

And with day, cloud chambers,
blue light ushering us to work,
the great milk-stained skies youth walks under.

Prolific, until the transport rolls up and
breaks the truce, and, full of hearted fervour,
names the victim, collapsing the sky props,
turning the black domino on its side.

Calipers and wedges. The future.
Poisoned the fields, and the sea,
slaughtered the livestock, only
Africa survived, singing
"I'm on the road again."
And the past widens before us, saying
It is love, it is love, that breaks the world.
But I wouldn't hesitate,
at any price.

Crucefix and lamp niche
solitary spirit in temporary accomodation
at home with the lynx and the bear.

Dark, you came and sat beside me
I lost half my wing, on waking
the sky was a dome in the rock, the wren
screamed past its entrance.

The hired men, bashing at the rock face
and walking back to the villages, singing
slow old songs. I believe
passionately that steady work
to a cleared purpose is true love.
The wren knows it exactly,
the moth expiring in *éclat*
no one called it art.

Cave wall crumbled into human form
arms outspread and the world is restored
to what it is, children playing in the square
under the coloured lights, thumb-nail
turning the screw-head.

Sings love into the roads and
up the steps and over the threshold
of the house, where we sleep each other's sleep
and mark to the inch the star measure
in the neighbour's eye.
And pray, and demand, to be
thus, at least.

No it is not granted. Doherty on the roads of Donegal,
wind and rain, a fiddle in a sack on his back. Arabia
howls. Tuning the earth.

By the thin light, watched
by the dead man, writing
new words in the old book.

The travellers' wagon passes over the brow
singing, scattering words into the fields.
Clown father pushes syllables together like
plug and socket, belches and falls asleep in the hay.

Gender merchant, with icy breath, love
hesitates. But knows no other inclination.

Years fighting bureaucracy, and finds
love is an ordered thing, requiring
good light for reading at night, little midges
squirming on the desk top.

There is a knock at the door. A small boy
stands there. "I have nowhere to go.
I'm hungry and I'm cold."
O steakeating modernists, the lamp

dims and fails. Slowly, over centuries
the fourth estate advances. And what
am I then?

Desk top, death top. Sandstone inlier
yielding readily to the chisel, a watchpoint
over the trade routes, guarded by a stranger.

To retire, to turn
face from world, ashamed to weep so,
being a king.

And those who return in the evening
know death is debated in caves in far
crannies of the forest hill, and nod so.
And grip the spade like a sceptre.

The stone man
sees all, the light livens his
frown, concealing the vast
animal resource, the golden wings
buried in the frown.

Everyone's wings, the wings of everyone,
shadowing the plain, descending on the hill,
the accusation, of the great wings, Yes,
you meant well, but did not open and beam.

Indeed I did not, I harboured resentment,
the children irritated me. But I go gladly.
Lay your last feather on me
like a dolmen cap
as the army rounds the bend.

So the image gets erased,
hope sunk into rock,
grasped.

We go but we shall be back, we shall
return here. Everything will be
as it was before the war. Walk up the steps
and enter the house. Same old
address, same postcode, same subsidence.
Say hello at the bar, yes, we're back.

The world is peeling apart but
it'll be over, and we shall be back, sporting
the uniform in which death is dressed.

Butterfly on the lemon balm,
gentle drumming, my
worst fears, my sweet rest.

SECOND SETT

Heaps of fruit piled up against the houses
grandfathers piled up in the ground
churchyard fruit, pears, cherries
travellers selling small bags of hazels

If all the world is to go the same way—
all one empire, all serving the one broker?—
a thin sigh in the fields, baby
where did our love go?

The house in the fields
breathes, its timbers
flex in the night changes,
the star wheels churn

Piles of apples outside in the yard
yellow and red in separate heaps
slowly, under careful control
rotting into the music.

And all our promises
                    Dim light beaming
into the dark street through a doorway
shadows passing, many shadows, blurred
into the night and the soil of the road

Kindling stacked up in the yard
quiet talking behind the wooden fence
shadows passing like smoke in the street—
familiar journeys across the town: questions,
about seeds, electricity bills, the exact wording
of a fourth verse, carried from door to door

Shield us from the arm in the sky
the glittering scar badges
when the hand drops the cash

Partners, workmates, door
to door, guard your
hope, columns of shade.

Guard your offer, the trust that spreads through the towns,
the open door, the carved double arc
catching the shadow at morn and eve.
Strangers welcomed, departures wept, a
real town.

I, or whoever this language pauses at,
pause again, where the railway crosses the road,
the slow fire threaded through lives
the aromatic smoke above the roofs
the dusty hands that hold hope forth

Meadow light on the iris
and the microscope and the bauble, turning
the market calendar, shunting the days,
the door that stays open.

Late afternoon, a layer of wood smoke
hanging over the village
like something asleep

Over in "the developed world"
the corporate voice dries to a hiss.
A vicious hiss.

And in all this country, these thousands of households
there is an annual fair of all the pitches of the heart
house to house in sub-zero temperatures the true love
chalice is brought with singing, clear, direct, locked
in its form, echoed from the hard earth. It is
the only corporate voice. The only defence.
The red cusp at its centre.
The rest is a dry hiss.

Stratum of wood smoke, pale blue over
the village roofs, the beasts
returning from the fields
walk down the street, turning
each into its own yard

We thrust our hands into dirt and grease
and fray them against rope, but we
hold the crown of the years, it is we
who sew the calendar into the sky

Night arrives, the smoke disperses, the sky clears
and the plough, the great plough above
signifying nothing now,
but a far greater nothing
than any president

I thought so, in the small room
made of wood,
the flies veer to the light.

In the stillness an evidence, plain
there in the air above us,
brother, sister

Mud on your shoes
standing still in the tides
of expansion, and the wreck
of the communal tone—
markets strung on fear

Your steady patient walking, sibling,
in the rain, among fruit trees
and dark haystacks, laughing
at the new rhythm.

A ceiling, translucent, over
our anxieties and calm,
someone walking by the river, casting
a shadow into the air above

The anxieties knitted into our calm,
us someones, walking under our thoughts,
the light hovering where we stoop

We stress the condition
but the fruit is continual

Leaning against the wall

Old man with a little plum-wood flute.

Curtains of onions and maize strung up
on the verandas to dry, the smoke rising when they
fire the yard ovens in the late afternoon
for tomorrow's bread

The car mechanic sits on the doorstep drinking beer,
the mountain behind him turns black.
He is the mechanic of all moving things
he is not in a hurry and he doesn't want to be paid.
The mountain is wooded to the top.

The work lies there like a song, waiting.
The lives sing their completions, constantly
infolded resolution, daily work
of the whole valley, singing out tomorrow's fear.

The white smoke layered over where and when,
over the name, and the day, over all of us.

In that day the renewed agreement,
the empty river bed full of red leaves
winding down the pastures among
haystacks, and small trees full of
small red apples and no leaves . . .

Yes, we are willing to stay around
for a while. We believe.

And say, good night, noapte buna,
smoke rising to the star base.

Columns of smoke rising
from the 5 o'clock fires
all over the valley, tomorrow's loaves
waiting like moons, like slow clocks.

Roads of wet earth between the houses.
"Look at this miserable place I live in,
look at this mud, this filth."

Look at us, developed, perfectly smooth,
perfectly dry. Heart,
where did our bombs go?

Our love, our bombs,
our lovely bombs. Our contradictions
waiting like mines, like slow clicks.

Open land, then forest, then air.

Leonardo Bruni said that the harmonious
workings of the institutions of Florence
derived from the beauty *and geometry*
of the Tuscan landscape.

A thin track, a line in the grass across
the pastures and over the riverside humps
everywhere worked, the shape of the place
carved from work, lines curving to meet,
leading ultimately homewards.

The forest walking backwards
far away that other land
green eye in the branches—*this fear*
protects our children from our success,
and the astronomy from our failure.

I am nothing to this place, a
hole in it. But the tears they cry with
reach my lip

Compatriots of the unimportant spaces
slow backs that bears the entire geometry
carrying the can to the bar, mending
the bicycle, tuning the viola,
as the hills swell into night again
and another wedding tilts
the earth into sense.

(Dawn Song)

Evidently, the world, and
the pine twig, the process.
I have held this hope for years.

A pain to the left of the stomach
another behind the thigh,
hair that was once black as night

Will I lean into you
at midnight, will I
see you from a grey fortress

On the long worked land
washed in rain
not looking back.

CODA

14 POEMS

THE TOWNS ALONG THE TISA

O the towns along the Tisa, the flaking walls, the ragged squares, Habsburg halls and communist concrete eroding in the river wind. Border towns stuck with closed borders, broken bridges over the Tisa, holes in the roads, buffalo carts ignoring the traffic lights. A shepherd with staff and cloak stands outside the Hotel Tisa, gypsies in orange skirts and wide-brimmed black hats cluster on corners. People wandering the streets hoping to pick up some work or leaning against walls on market day holding in front of their midriffs the one object they've got for sale, a model house or a packet of tea. The last offices in the west, heated by small woodstoves, desks heaped with impractical directives, as the first bits of snow descend and everything gets dark together.

KALOTASZEG

Low hills carved into terraces
neglected now, wild grass. Trans-
sylvanian air, a music
as of saddened royalty

Who became migrant workers, drivers
of long-distance lorries
with the same patience, the same
gateway, sun and rope

Moon and string, we forget slowly
the star's aim on the bare hills,
remember in a different script
the answer of the heavy beast
snorting behind the gate.

Consequence at world pace,
slower than the death birds.

THE CROWD YELLED OUT FOR MORE

Suddenly, in a cellar bar in Oradea badly heated in late October coats on waiting for dinner, a few young people drinking beer and the Romanian edition of Who Wants To Be A Millionaire on the screen behind us with nobody paying any attention—they should know, the uselessness, of riches to poverty—

I realised what was coming out of the speakers was A Whiter Shade of Pale, Procul Harum, 1968. I was alone again, Andrew Crozier was leaning over the billiard table in a pub in St. Leonards. I was recently married, I was doing summer language teaching. The future was something completely different from what we now inhabit. It was all over, the death-dealing state, blasting the necessary outsider, the furious rage that maintains vast privilege it was finished, we had hope we had normality before us. I was back in my cell, quietly singing the nonsense.

Pilliszántlaszló

Forest paths in Autumn
columns of sky "heavenly blue" between
brown trees with orange leaves

The wind moving slowly
through the tree tops
on long legs.

FRUSTOVENTO

The wind walks the grass. Bee orchids, crickets.
The good, solid house, the stone house on
a platform rising from the brush of the hillside
under Monte Subasio. Clover, trickling water.
The closed house, platform for an angel's foot.

An angel from the paintings over the hill. Voices
gently in the ear of the mind, negociating
a temporary pact with the gravities of the world.
Crotchet of green leaf chained to the solar system
where the angel's foot descends, and lightly rests

For a moment. On a roof tile, or neatly avoiding
a buttercup, and is gone. Does the hero's heart
burn for something grander? Or the earth beg release
from hearts with no time for such smallnesses?
Begs and pleads, for the tear to fall as due.

SCHIELE

The skin also marked
where the foot landed
or the tear fell, touched
blue and green, faint
bruising, thin membrane
letting through
the shades of society. Eyes
staring out in alarm.

STUCK IN VIENNA FOR TWO WEEKS WATCHING CNN EVERY NIGHT

Of course we inhabit decisions not made by us
or anyone we can trace, decisions threaded into
the streets and forests from impossible distance.

Forget Tuesday, forget Vietnam,
day to day, door to door,
bomb first, forget later.

Walk the streets, forgotten children,
dust of burning villages on your shoes
walk the forests, learn to live.

In this house
Franz Schubert wrote
An die ferne geliebte baby,
was our love ever with us?

And these clean streets
not made by us, this
integral distance, the ghosts
that walk it.

Room 40, Früstuckepension Caroline, Gudrunstrasse 138, Wein 9

The courtyard tree swaying in the wind.
If the business is still going strong
how can you bear to die? If the space
owned is cleansed of failure, the walls
impeccably bare, the one tall tree reaching
beyond the courtyard roofs and so
catching the wind, how can anyone
bear to live? What is there to forget?

As if every block didn't proclaim a history,
the pink arches, the eagles with straight wings,
the world's savagery always ready.

Withered flowers.
You are rest and peace.

A Cold Room in Granada

A voice calling in English under the trees
of the square. Already they are going
for their newspapers. She has
arrived safely, go back to sleep.
The news ends where the story begins.

And we shall dress our minds
in all the hope of the story—
the hill covered in white houses,
the long story, the carefully turned
corner of alabaster holding a piece of light.

The measuring wheel, carefully turned,
the electric fire hung on a coat-hook
the water as it flows over the sculpted edge
agreement between things and people
the trees at night full of birds.

Chattering heart, turn finally
to the end of the story in clear cold light:
the moment achieved, snow on marble,
people living in caves, singing
bodies fruit and die.

Terezín

The world stands. Visitor, reader,
be quiet, learn to die. Lover of sleep,
learn to fall, into a small space
with a plaque on the wall saying: HERE . . .
This place, this grassy ground where it swells
here against the wall. Was brought here.
And forty thousand more, one by one.

Sang, danced, acted here. Worked,
as people must. Killing work. Nobody
is disqualified from the duties compassion
exacts, nobody is privileged by this suffering
and the vastness of resource it sets in motion.
Vast Europe, breaking circuit at a small
garrison town the mountains in the distance

The mountains in the distance, breaking Europe
across a small child's arm. The small child left
a crayon drawing and what the drawing said was,
Agree to suffice, not to surpass, agree to be
the actual person, nothing else will break
the circuits of plunder. The drawing was of
two beds and a coat hanger.

After Terezín

So on the bus back, mountains
in the distance, fading fields

Compassion without privilege or guilt
peace over Judaea

The stars signing their
light into shrines in the desert

O that your state power
were buried in those shrines.

The bus rattles, I hum
songs to my bones.

Withered flowers, you are
sense, you are light.

Alstonefield, after Dinner

Leaving the George Inn to walk down
the small road to Milldale
it is so quiet as the light diminishes
pale things begin to glow on the ground

Each tree makes a slight whispering
bats flit overhead, gnat
attempts to enter nostril—solitary,
you are free to let your emotions expand.

Light sinks into the downy slopes, turning
green to silver. Someone has chalked
DAD HURRY UP on the steepest
part of the road, and this grand

Sense expands, towards
people living in their structures
everywhere against each other
in a common fall

Turning at the day's end
into the movement of the earth.
Entering sleep, knowing nothing,
the one moment free of harm.

Across Central Europe

How much more is there to add to what
we can never forget, and what
will happen to it in the end when all
the memory goes out like a light switched off?

Forest and mountain without end.
Night falls, clustered lights, of villages
and small towns on ridge tops or the sides
of big valleys, deepening green.

Ride on old car, bockwürst at the services,
snow squalls, what *is* the future of memory?—
keep it rolling towards us, the road under
and the dark over, all coming down together
to the cathedral lights of Limburg.

AM WEIßE ROß

To shine in your eyes like
the cathedral lights of Limburg.

And in the morning watch the frost
rising from the river.

Afterword to *Two*
Setts and Coda

Sett means the same as *Suite*, a number of things put together in a particular order, for a purpose or to form a whole. In this spelling it suggests to me the ardour and resource of a particular phase of English instrumental dance music in the 17th Century, involving the renewal of musical material as it passes from one piece to another through different forms and metrics.

Sett One is subtitled: *Meditations on the Hermit's Cave at Cratcliffe Tor, near Winster, Derbyshire.* This is a small cave at the foot of a sandstone cliff in a wood, with a recognisably 15th Century crucifix carved in the wall, along with a stoup and a bench. It would have been inhabited by a professional hermit, trading for alms in coin and kind against prayers for people's souls and the safety of travellers, for it was close to a major trade route.

Sett Two is subtitled: *Meditations on the villages of the Mara Valley, Maramures, Romania.* This area has been described (inaccurately) as "the last true peasant society left in Europe."

The subtitle of the Coda is: *Westward across central Europe in an old Renault Espace indulging serial breakdowns, fleeing winter, with interventions from other travels.* That was in October 2001.

It sometimes helps to know these, and it sometimes helps to forget them.

NOTES

Sett One

Hierusalem is how Jerusalem was spelled in the Latin Vulgate and thus in church music. "Jerusalem, return to thy God" became a refrain of settings of the Lamentations of Jeremiah.

"Ten thousand years, drinking of the wine" is from a net-hauling song sung by The Menhaden Chanteymen, and is a figure of paradise.

"The heard heart breaks, the wax heart melts" is quoted from a Hungarian Transylvanian "dawn song" sung by Márta Sebestyén with Muzsikás.

Sett Two

"Where did our love go? . . . and all our promises" *Baby Love*, Diana Ross and The Supremes, 1964

noapte buna: Romanian for "good night."

Coda

Tisa or *Tisza:* The river separating northern Transylvania from Ukraine then running southwards through Hungary to join the Danube.

Kalotaszeg: Hungarian name for an area of west-central Transylvania.

Oradea: Town in Romania close to the border with Hungary.

Pilliszántlászlo. Village on the Danube Bend north of Budapest.

Frustovento: "a bit of a wind": an unoccupied house discovered in the hills north of Assisi in 1996.

Schiele: Egon Schiele, Austrian painter, 1890–1918.

Stuck in Vienna . . .

"An die ferne geliebte" (To the distant beloved) : The house was at Kahlenbergdorf and the notice on it said that Schubert wrote "Trockne Blumen" (withered flowers) there, but something in CNN news altered this. In fact Beethoven wrote An die ferne geliebte.

Room 40 . . .

"The pink arches, the eagles with straight wings" refers to (a) early 20th Century socialist or even Marxist inspired large-scale apartment housing which can still be seen in Vienna, (b) the imperial eagle as it was stylised during the Nazi period, still to be seen on some institutional buildings in Vienna.

Terezín or Theresienstadt:. Garrison town north of Prague used by the Nazis as a transit camp for deported persons, including children, on their way to the killing camps in Poland.

lover of sleep: the french poet Robert Desnos, who died at Terezín 18th June 1945, a few weeks after its liberation.

Across Central Europe . . .

bockwürst: boiled sausage.

Limburg: the one in Hessen, on the River Lahn.

Am Weiße Roß. At the White Steed. A pub and guest house in Limburg, overlooking the river. Recommended.

NOON PROVINCE

Jag sjunger om det enda som försonar,
det enda praktiska, för alla lika.

—Gunnar Ekelöf

THE NIGHT TRAIN
ARRIVES AT DAWN

Valuable small acts. Arriving
from the other side of the country
to the standard breakfast,
wanting an ordinary thing
that people believe in,
such as the day begins,
keeps them on and together—
a variety of travellers
neglecting in first light
stature or office . . .
Take your turn, ask only
for the complete, the integral.

Market Day at Apt

How it fills the town to its purpose,
stalls heaped with olives, cheeses,
chickens and doves, fills the squares
with food and clothing, the streets with
garlic and mushrooms, ordinary things
as we speak them, full of knowledge
and desire, crowds under plane trees,
sound of talking all through the town.
Cavern of image the mouth keeps its
tone, retains its modest expectation,
pulses in tune to the pocket,
the ordinary day that earns it.
Wild lavender honey from the hills.

Fragments at Les Bassacs (arriving)

(a)

A tower-house between sky and fields
with dust up to the door. It is
where we are, where we are
to be resolved

(b) (Peering over Barny's shoulder)

Scraping stones and pieces of earth
against cream paper you make
a drawing of the landscape,
curved into its resolution.
Its resistance. Its warning

(c)

Where are we?
I am witless, cannot invoke
curious detail, eye on the sky
on the dust

Les Bassacs (d)

The houses, fawn stone, red roofs, lean
into each other, backs to the expanse,
from the valley a fortress on a shelf,
bulging and flaking. We think we hear faint voices

In the ground and between the stones,
dealing and deciding in a lost language,
a far and fragile history, though no-one
passes this way any more. Us, we

Come and go. We form a company.
We take over a corner of the structure
and peer through a new high window
onto (a clear day) bright mountains

And distant sea light. It is our passion
to know how close we are, our pain
and principal, to take on the trade.
Any profit we make goes to the history.

Roofwatch

1.

Day and night the sky arches over
hills and plain turning against
the earth, clouds springing
from the dark wooded edge fan
over the farmed land and at
night the plethora of stars
turns clear and sure and
compact in their terraces
above a veiled and separated ground.
O fine in their farming the stars
rally and exit all night.

2.

Full adoration without question.
The white rock breaks on the wooded slopes
over there and the sun dies constantly
over the vinefields, burning out fruit.

Repletion without any question
and no curriculum to offer the world,
no credentials you would ever believe
for the sun burns cherries out of twigs

And the stars thresh mind pages
to a solitary and quiet wish
to line a space before we turn
to love's raging difference.

AFTERTHOUGHT

I take the lemonade bottle to the village
and get it filled with red wine (a litre)
improving (no doubt) the status of the object.

We proceed to fill ourselves.
But when we are full our generosity is only a meaning we have,
and the unfilled remains always more filling.

STUBBORN INTERVAL

I would like to be always present.
Not helpful or obedient
but there, without question
without sex without support
without supper or cigars
but without cease, again
as I am here, in this stone
stack of rooms at the foot
of the fields again and again.

For there needs to be a
(ordinary, unfilled, blue-green, etc.)
staying item, a point of
(salt wind pours over the sky)
(scouring wind)
stubborn answer.

St-Saturnin, the Ridge

We are entitled to neglect,
in the abandoned garden above the roofs
of the town we are guaranteed separation,
to squat under the shapely dark cypress
with you there and you there
eating black olives and taking photographs
the yellow broom throbbing in the wind
the lizards on the wall of the dry cistern
darting away, the films and ads of the
town deep in us: a politics of matching
by which we are neglected
and rightly so, calling us out
of defeat to the fruiting flesh.

Meditations in the Fields / 1

Strolling in the olive groves and
orchards, dry sky and hot stones, hard
light and Ockeghem on the walkman—
I time the intervals. They are tightly numbered
and of such extent, such meeting parts
that all the time I wasted in disuse
(bed, social time, infant fear)
and wasn't treading the mind's width
is reckoned to my regret and returned
untouched to the earth, or so it seems.

/2

Gazing at the ground
wild thyme and sparse grass
the blue bellflower, Aphyllanthus
Monspeliensis, hanging over the stones
between the cherry trees patches of sunlight
and Josquin in the earphone I
am sold out. We receive everything
and return it, in the flesh.
Now because it is charted. The flesh
fruits so fulsome and glad precisely
as farmed, didn't they say?

/3

Pausing in the hot vine fields, Brumel
through the wire seeming to say
that mutual enemies debate in the
chambers of the heart, as Dante
certainly said, and a small spirit
pleads to the soul through a thin wire:
Regain your place. And sweet and low
(as thyme fills the air) O scouring focus
neglect our substance if you will but
shepherd this instant to its kingdom as only
the sharpened spirit kens and quickly—
Shew mercy on those good shepherd on
us ourselves, the very ones who
sit alone for their receipt in a foreign field
send us to our remembrance, it's time
clear enough through the crackle and fuzz
death's silence leading each tone
onwards, to lock the door
and fall into human length.

THE WALK TO ROUSSILLON

The red cliff in the dark green woods,
walk towards it. As you get
closer it is difficult to see.

LINES AT NIGHT / 1

Back at evening, a stone room full
mainly of fireplace. We burn
olive roots, dry thyme, as night
gathers outside we finish
the wine, foot on sill.

Everything we touch grates
with dust and the fire
crackles and flares up.
The fire dies down, the fields
outside are gradually closed.
A speaking darkness surrounds us

And you are in it, and the light
you hold in there, is that a belief?
What else could it be?

Lines at the Pool
above St.-Saturnin

Alpine swift (the white chested) carving the air
and a quick wind from the hills redolent of
pine and lavender rides the rocky cleft
skimming the surface our sight remains
unpolitically tabulated / innocent in delight.
It is perfectly right, forswearing a life
fixed in ratio to demand like a permanent
insect-target for the flashing creature.
All we ask is that the heads of the town
read justice faithfully.

What do we know of world and detail who can't
compete with the swift for vantage in the
dream of earth? That speed of gain and grace
leaves us standing, lost in our weight and
hesitance, lost in delight at the fruitless sight
of the species pilot fixing history to a dive.

But delight closes and light rises. The limbs
tremble and bow to the mind that pokes
the blazing episphere of day at its fault
facing world torsion with what? with a politeness,
a reasonable plea: *Raste Krieger, Krieg ist aus.**
Beautiful silent answers move over the hills.

So among ruined walls and broken arches
we foreswear a hope that has no substance
set sticks on bricks, gather truthful items from
the surrounding area and algebraize a sequence.

Later the lake dims, the birds retire
the mind or something silently similar
hovers in plagal trust in the crumbling air,
talking to death at the ancient gate
where the locust pauses, and the woody stalk.

*"Hold it, soldier. War is out."

Meditations in the Field /4

Anywhere in the world the
mind wakes while I
contemplate a field corner and now
Lassus in the speaker telling
of a rose entrammelled in the years,
surviving as so much else
continues to exist, so much
pain and disappointment
the rose we make again, that you would
never recognise or credit as that same
Armonia, that unfolding, clad in
the regency of the moment—
a silent and remote
fold in the edge of the hills
where a few things grow and I
harvest exclusive result.

Lines at Night /2

Evening cloaks the ground again
and here we are in that stone room, table,
chairs, fireplace, dusty lightbulb, slightly
cooler air. And really not
trying too hard. Up on
the roof terrace five
large bats dip through
the small zone of electric light.

Thick night, lit windows,
and punctured sky. Who
lives here and what they believe
(television, future, mask)
is held against harm
lightly if we trust the opening cluster.
And who knows? It's warm enough
to sleep on the roof.

LACOSTE

The landscape is a thought thing,
it has been thought as a gift and as a burden.
We drive through someone's book to
the Marquis de Sade's castle, where misthought
has left not a trace.

House prices flutter and electronic pastoral
beats the air to no result: the true architecture
speaks only *vulgare illustre,* heartstuff,
dialect/reduction/vantage stand flat to the side,
everything except justice is an impertinence.

It is a crowned structure, a hill
rearing to intellect and lust as a burden
patiently and proudly borne, set
clear above the fruiting plain
brighter stone than star because thought
                                        flawed

Recalling Lacoste
(lines at night /3)

Back at night in an old room,
total country silence. Dim bulb,
moth at window, bread and cheese
Côtes du Rhone Beaumes de Venise 1985
cheap but delicately heartening.
Silent tonight, reading a pocket
guide or Dante and thinking of home.

The castle ringed the summit in white, the village
houses were its skirts trailing into the ridged fields.
One does what one can, of course, but only
what we know we do does much good.
The village dog barks twice and stops. Thin
noise of someone's music. There is
a question always at hand, sometimes a horror,
which we are entitled to neglect, with
courtesy. And could do much
more but look at the time.

Escape from our Uncaring

Mid-day heat at the ochre quarries.
We have pulled the earth aside and left
ourselves without shadow, without
that dark doubt that saves us.

And stamp on in absolute certainty:
£8,000,000 for a Van Gogh.
("No cost is too high").

Returning to the fields, the dark cherries
are dying to be pulled. In the village
the new bread swells and cracks.

Up the Big Hill and
Back by Ten

Walking the mind, walking the prosody,
uphill, hour upon hour on a stone track
through the garrigue and straight up the hot hill.
It is numbered. The little oaks whisper,
the numbers are there whatever you do
or say, no rests or interludes, sheer calm
continuing as the numbers last, when
the numbers are full you are there. No one
in. A bright green lizard on a stone.

So we turn, descend, count on. A wasps' nest
up a tree, a mantis' egg-sac under a stone.
Unkempt mountain lavender fields,
thyme, alkanet, early purple orchid,
remote farms up in the hills where much more
than entire lives have been played out and love
has been doubled or quartered and time clicks.

Politics is a play of fear. Fearful
clicking of time in the hills as if
a life is never enough meaning. It is
more than enough. A book in my pocket
by Dante, a pocket edition. When we get back
we'll have bread and cheese with wine
and count the day to its figured close.

COUNTING THE COST
(SYLLABLES AT NIGHT)

We are back and silent, no
fire tonight, dull light
of the moony bulb, the door
latched, the shutters to.

Count the silence: seven five
count the silenced, oh
millions, lost in the sky and
scattered on the earth

Never to be spoken or
known by any name
whose continuity is
with us in the night

Night of other nights
when we were silent
and the earth turned ahead of
our silent petrified thought.

Teaching us to be nothing
in distant foreign corners
the earth turns the dark
into truth. Wait there.

THE WALK BACK TO GORDES (LINES)

OR

RESOLUTION AND INTERDEPENDENCE

We are together we are lost
in dazzling light in the limestone
gullies and terraces of a complicated hill
in a blaze of flowering shrubs. Taking
goat paths between drystone walls
stooping under laden branches stepping
among swallowtails we find our way
together and what does it ever mean
but action and purpose, to be together?
A stupid simple thing to say as if
destruction were not also action and purpose
and being lost among flowers.
We must get back and think ourselves
carefully apart and trade our love limb
for limb. As the swallowtails swarm.
As the dying flare.

NUMBERS AT LES CROAGNES

Reaching for food
offered I disappear
into a vetch stratum.
Stay with me, guilt
is a square plot,
an abandoned garden
or olive grove
in front of a chapel
with a locked door.
We say nobody seems
to mind. Soft wine
raises our spirits to
the foliation band.
Whoever says he minds
will be offered a glass.

Just a Song (lines at night /5)

Dusk on the upper fields, the bushes
and small trees clumps of blackness
in a grey haze. The walker, alone, has
slight but simple script to find his path,
streaks of paleness on the ground. The moon
encloses the air, the bullfrog creaks
in the silence, the grasses fidget and lapse.

He listens to the silence and hears
nonsense, eyeless jokes in a dark hall.
His mind runs ahead of it becoming
leader of a quiet procession
trailing down the hillside between fields
holding the moon on the end of a stick

To see his way. The message is clear
and hopeful. His best intentions mesh
with the world's world and fall back towards
his interclusion and so they must
or Death gets double six and an extra go
because the littleness of his world succeeds.
Look how he hangs from the moon!

The path leads clearly down to the edge
of the slope and rejoins the road where
it hangs over the wide valley scattered
with house lights and a steady glow
from behind the far hills. Someone has left
an old white horse in a field with food
water and shelter, standing through the night.

NOTES ON THE ATTEMPT TO VISIT LORAND GASPAR

I want to bring in everything but
the poem wants to leave everything out
and where does that get us? Dialing numbers,
getting recorded messages to say there is
no reply. Driving an orange car
on ribbon roads over the hills between
the orchards to the coastal marshes,
white horses grazing in the grey flats,
the poem tapping its foot on the
accelerator and coughing for more
fuel, wanting to get on with the work,
wanting to move, out, across the city
in fits and starts, looking left and right
for a cathedral or a telephone exchange,
Gabrieli on the car radio saying there are
beams and levers at every point of the continuance.
And so we roll into the village square
and park in the motley of plane leaves, too
hot and dazzled to speak the language.
Where on earth is the man with the orange poem?

The Slower Walk to Roussillon with Kathy

Walking through the fields, not to create
harm that devolves back to worlds.
A black cricket with orange knees, beaming
yellow furze, a white butterfly with black
edging and sage underwing. Listen

While I tell you. Blue iris newly unwrapped,
when you're nearer to death than birth
the coin begins to pass more openly
like the earth at a good conjunction.
A five-pointed violet star.

Then the wheatfield bloody with poppies.
I think this swelling bright horizon
holds us (passing) at our best yet
since we don't know where final justice lives
and death isn't quite enough to meet the need for it

We care desperately to create a good
past us, taking to risk an edge of harm.
In a sudden hot hollow a mass of brown
butterflies and round the corner an
orange car containing.

THE TELEPHONE BOX ON THE EDGE OF THE CORNFIELD

Letters and numbers spray from our minds,
settle on the wires in unbroken code. The car
sees everything with two hollow eyes
sees there is nothing to see but signs
at choices. This is what our minds
are reduced to, living in this world.

So we get out and stand by the field leaning
on the box and light breezes play the
corn like Mbira. There is red and slight
blue undertext, disclosed where least
expected from time to time.

And the heart is said to be a
rare blue object in a red matrix
surrounded by the yellow goods.
Consuming and lashing strokes. On the
border of which a mind or surface
pauses, keeping all this together.

Last Night

(1)

Stretched in the stone chamber
awake and listening
to the dark stone silence that
grew from nothing. Final justice
lives in our hearts.

And nothing here is ours, we came
and went like a night moth, a few
tourists were here for a week
they stayed up late in thought by
the single lamp.

Exactly so, exactly us
fishing for quick messages
in the wind along the wall,
histories of earth that signal
to the whole heart

That the world is there out there
in the dark full of hope and
silence and calling to a
centre. A single bell rings
across the valley.

Slowly the heart unfolds, slowly
the mind weighs. Ordinary events
that hold people together and
on into day and year in
spite of loss.

Helpful and obedient too,
passing faithful to the
substance that writes itself
across the night and back to our
lives in the end.

(2)

Sensing a power that
answers death I move to the
window and nothing happens.
"A beautiful and gentle wild thing
pierces my breast"

And turns there and chambers and
libraries fan out from that
simple point and a music
farms the air. How it
bells the close!

And we are cast against
injustice in wild longing,
screw our eyes at the world which
won't settle into peace until
it is far too late it is over.

There is nothing but darkness out there
and something flies out, some creature
of breath, over the hill calling
and calling like to like
one power to one life.

As if a person could do a thing
but inhabit a language that makes sense
whose periods follow themselves in
tune to distance and arrive
ahead of harm.

Something in the dark quiet
night whispers in my head after
tearing my breast and tells me look there is
nothing there, there is no
rose but truth unfolding

(3)

Light and substance. We are caught
in a tangle of seeking
consequence. And the winner
weeps at his success, to have taken on
earth's thankless gain.

Refuse it. Act on the very
minim of reluctance and the city
rears behind the hill—
calm terraces, theatre
of entire lives where flesh

Unfolding turns at last
to shore, to earth's arc, bright
moon on the tree jagged edge of the
black hill out there for a moment
which is a moment

Of complete certainty never to be
relinquished; heart infoliate the only
lasting or wanted thing.
And the stream running under the wall
and the paling ash

We leave behind, shoulder
luggage and are forgotten.
Leaving an empty house, the night
bird perched on the roof ridge
pealing death out

Of hiding, out of the horizon.
Then a slight paling begins, night
turns and trots down the valley, dreams
wrapped in darkness and world
break into day.

ORANGE TO CHARTRES

Stay and work, stay and work,
build machines in the garden.
The leaf opens to show a chrysalis.
A tortoise suddenly crosses the path.
Oh stay anyway, work to the planet's
demand: how to pan that mothering arc
away from worlds to here, and come
to know at some impossible distance
how love comes finally to a start.

A model of the heart, standing
across the river. It shines at night,
covered in creations and justices,
opercular, a closed work, that stands
there like an old man in the sun—
a message of arcaded days, shadowed access
to what we are. And can and will.
Loved justly because a credit succeeds us.
At which the star leaps into the rose.

Slow Meditation in the Café-Bar *Les Caves du Mont Anis*, le Puy

Sometimes a feeling comes on me saying that to love the very savour of human being is such a rare thing, to love a kind of savour or centre of what we are, which is an ordinary thing but the only truth we wholly know, the only fullness without interference, our own stake in time: the person being here. That is not a sudden or dramatic thing, that does not imply wide revelation, but is here all the time. And on rare occasions we notice, that there is a truth at our pivot, that it fans out through us, that we can act and speak on its tide.

And it is never quite singular, you know, never quite alone, however much we shirk the focus there is always that telling chime; to sit alone in a cave under the cathedral is to smile at a library of honesty. And welcome what we can of it. We can hardly move without that prime informer the tongue across time and worlds funnelled down onto what we perceive and learn. We cannot even guess at the weight and pressure of true souls informing a slight movement of the lower lip, a faint stirring at the back of the head moving towards language, a feeling as of the slow dropping of veils, the narrowing of world light to an entrance.

This feeling says very little, it says only that the light is not yet out and every point in the world continues to exist as every person who ever did exist had a centre which transmitted itself into a vocabulary and on into hope. Even those, I think, who preferred hurt. But it is a feeling which occurs in a pause and protected from both sides, protected and fuelled by the days and futures of searching, obedient, action. Protected from what anybody ever did by what they might. We cannot arrange for such pauses.

It says a little more too, in a kind of weariness inhabiting the resilience and ease of the feeling, almost an edge of anger to the blissful prescience like a line of shadow marking the edge of an arch. It mentions that we also hate this life and all its distracting obstacles. It says that the angels, in the tympanum, with their serrated wings, are more beautiful and more human than the dark twisted flesh of our comedians and newscasters because they also assure us that we are also not here, also not anywhere on this striven planet at all, we have already come to an end and a line and a syllable mark out the wonderful pleasure of not having to be where we are put, not having to be here in this lying cave. One window opening onto a stone wall. That is to say, this is not a mixed feeling, but a feeling with an edge.

This block of sense is beyond harm while it stays. Its tranquil inwardness offers goodness indirectly, as the world understands, shadowed in honour and fidelity, starting with those we know best. For it exhorts us to declare ourselves in full. And at an enjoining of calm by which the offer must be repeated until it is taken, falling again and again to lay the coin at your feet, to make verses. Craftily glossing the past into trust via forgetting it rather precariously opens the future through its own delicately poised moment and totally assures the hesitant bearer: *the end is in sight,* minutely, so slight it almost hurts to locate. And what is your secret then in the years to come of elsewhere and departure, what does it matter then to have gained a self rise? It is returned anyway, the earth wants it all back. Stay with what you are. Work the burden and blind fear out of continuance by no more than a noticed edge, a flicker of grass, a simple attendance—that is, to shepherd this moment to its kingdom, as we have slowly learned in centuries of script. The continuance held in the instant and helpless out of it, like a lost child. And that is to say, I know nothing but this table. On which is represented by curious skill, a pattern of welfare. A pattern of warfare. A map of faring.

AFTERWORD TO *NOON PROVINCE*

Most of these poems were drafted in an eccentric stone house in a small hamlet called Les Bassacs, near St. Saturnin d'Apt, in Provence, in 1987. It was late spring, and a time of clear hot and windy weather, with episodes of dense opacity in the late evenings, as if each day closed by wrapping itself round you. The occasion was the first time I lived together with the children of both my marriages.

Almost all places named or unnamed are in the vicinity of this hamlet or represent day trips out from it, except those involved in getting there (by train to Avignon) and leaving (by car, Orange to Chartres via Le Puy). But in *Last Night* Les Bassacs is conflated with a small village on a hilltop in Languedoc called Usclas du Bosc, visited in May 1988, which had the sharper valley with wooded ridge, clear moonlit night, church clock and nightingale required for this piece.

NOTES

Epigram: "I sing of the only thing that reconciles, only of what is practical, for all alike."

Meditations in the Fields: these poems figure wandering in the fields around the hamlet listening to music through a personal stereo system. Ockeghem, Josquin, Brumel and Lassus are all European composers of (mainly) church music for choir in the 15th and 16th Centuries. They are placed in order of seniority in the four poems, Lassus being the youngest. The liturgical pieces, whose texts entered into the poems, were—Ockeghem: Mass for the Dead, Josquin: Stabat Mater, Brumel: O Domine Iesu Christe pastor bone, Lassus: not recorded.

Lines at the Pool Above St.-Saturnin. "Raste kriege . . ." Sir Walter Scott, from *The Lady of the Lake,* translated by Adam Storck and set by Schubert as *Ellens Gesang I.* Scott wrote, "Soldier rest! thy warfare o'er."

The Telephone Box . . . Mbira is the name of an east African musical instrument and the music it produces, which is steadily pulsating.

Escape from our Uncaring. Ochre is still used to make all colours of paint, but the quarries are almost entirely abandoned. Van Gogh's territory was not very far away, to the south-west beyond the hills on the other side of the valley. "No cost is too high" was spoken by an American president at the time, in support of which exploitative war I can't remember.

Last Night (2) "A beautiful and gentle wild thing . . ." is a lost quotation, I think from a 16th or 17th Century Italian poet.

www.ingramcontent.com/pod-product-compliance
Lightning Source LLC
Chambersburg PA
CBHW032018090426
42741CB00006B/651